LIFE ON THE STOOP

PHIL BRACCO

LIFE ON THE STOOP

Cover design and layout by Jamie Pelaez (www.JamiePelaez.com)

Edited by Robbie Bracco and Jamie Pelaez

INTRODUCTION

With the passing of time, life as we lived it during the early years in the old neighborhood at 190 Hamilton Avenue, in the Red Hook section of Brooklyn, New York as we knew it could be lost forever, if not recorded and shared.

These wonderful childhood experiences all transpired at what is now the entrance to the Brooklyn Battery Tunnel. While traveling through the tunnel, one would never know the fun, the hardships and the human emotions of the childhood we experienced within the confines of that small area known as Red Hook. I have shared these experiences in illustration form and each has a special tale to tell. I sincerely hope that you enjoy them as much as I have enjoyed sharing them with you.

I can honestly say that I had the greatest childhood of any person who ever lived on the planet and I have been truly blessed.

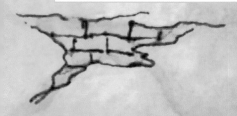

DEDICATION

In an era when women were confined mostly to the home and the raising of children, my grandmother was a pioneer who owned and operated her own neighborhood business. I grew up in two houses which she owned - one on Hamilton Avenue and the other on Second Place in the Red Hook section of Brooklyn. In addition to the homes she also owned a building on Union Street which was and still is a famous New York eatery even today. If you find yourself in my old neighborhood, be sure and visit "Ferdinando's Focacceria Restaurant". It is a true old fashioned experience. As a young boy I often accompanied my Grandmother to Union Street to collect the rent.

Grandma came to this country before the turn of the century and faced an uncertain life as she adjusted to a new world with a language she did not understand. Grandma worked in New York and took the ferry from Brooklyn to New York which cost a penny each way. She would then walk to the factory where she worked on Canal Street. She often told us the story of losing her penny which her father gave her for the ferry boat for getting back home after her hard days work in the sewing factory where she was able to secure work based on her skills as a dress maker which she had learned in Italy. Young brides would simply show her a picture of a gown they liked and she could construct it by creating her own pattern. Thanks to the generosity of a man at the ferry she was able to get back home that night.

Out of 16 children, only 8 survived due to extreme hardships and influenza. My father was the oldest with three brothers and four sisters. From her struggles and those eight children emerged Hollywood actors, Entrepreneurs, Attorneys, Doctors, War Heroes, Artists, Athletes and many other walks of life, down-to-earth people.

Hard times are not always bad for they can build character. I feel fortunate to have grown up in a family who taught responsibility, love, respect and honor. We should never be ashamed of humble beginnings. I would not trade mine for all the riches in the world.

PHIL BRACCO

This area of Red Hook was the hub of our community activities. The streets were filled with people coming and going. Whatever a family needed could be obtained right there in that neighborhood surrounding Columbia and Union Streets.

There were bakeries, butchers, dry goods, mattress shops, trunks and luggage, tailors, food peddlers, shoe stores, movie theatres, photographers, candy stores and an endless array of mom and pop shops where each person could display and sell their specialty wares. Everything imaginable was brought to our door by horse-drawn wagons which would bring the ladies down from their apartments to get the freshest foods available for their families.

I was always chasing the horse-driven wagons, trying to hang on to the back of each one. Occasionally, the driver would have to stop and chase all of us kids away for our safety. The sound of horseshoes clinking and clanking on the cobblestone streets are still vivid in my mind, which seems like yesterday, even after all of these years.

(Years later, when I was married with my own family, we moved to New Jersey and had a swimming pool built in our yard, but the lure of those days remained with me forever as I was able to collect truckloads of those old cobblestones as some of the streets were rebuilt and used them as a deck around our pool.)

On any given day one could find the old neighborhood men gathered on the corner sharing stories about several subjects. Their conversation would drift from which baseball team was the best or who was the greatest pitcher or home run hitter. "How about that Joe DiMaggio?" He was their hero AND he was Italian. Other times they might switch to politics or whose wife was the best cook. They could always find something to argue about and argue they did!

THE DAY THE FRUIT AND VEGETABLE HORSE RAN AWAY FROM THE WAGON

Like the residents of the neighborhood, the horses were confused about exactly what their role was during these uncertain times and this particular day the horse broke loose in an attempt to be free.

PLACING BOTTLE CAPS ON THE TROLLEY TRACKS
HAMILTON AVENUE | BROOKYLN, NY 1943

The reason for flattening them was so that we could use them as ammunition in our little toy wooden zip guns which we made from Orange crates.

This old photo of me shows the trolley tracks along Hamilton Ave and the entrance to where the Brooklyn Battery Tunnel is today at the end of the street as the construction for progress began and changed the lives of thousands of people who lived in that section of the Hook forever.

LISTENING TO GRANDPA'S ENDLESS FUNNY STORIES

Grandpa was a master at telling interesting stories and I was captivated and always hated for them to come to an end. I often wonder now, who was the most captivated — Me or Grandpa!

A tradition which I have tried to carry on with my own children and grandchildren.

FENCES, CARDBOARD BOXES AND GRAMMA'S CLOTHES LINE | BROOKLYN, NY

No one will ever know the countless hours we spent playing in my backyard as well as our neighbor's yards. All that our young minds could imagine would be acted out in this playground of ours. We were cowboys, Indians, Soldiers, Firemen and especially Superman! We could perform a truly great dying scene as we got shot and rolled in the soft brown dirt. We were always covered with dirt and our faces, legs and hands showed it.

Screams from my Grandmother, "don't pull the clothesline down," are still vivid in my memory today. We must have looked like large squirrels as we climbed everything imaginable - fences, drainpipes, poles and fire escapes.

Cardboard boxes were our clubhouses, caves, and hiding places and no outsiders were allowed in.

Such a simple way of life before children's imagination was lost with the invention of the TV and other modern inventions that compelled the youth to stay inside and so began the demise of many of the wonderful games and interactions of neighborhood life. The only electrical entertainment was the radio, which really opened up our minds because we could imagine anything we wanted to match what we heard emanating from that talking box. "I could see Superman flying thru the air and outrunning a speeding bullet, leaping over tall buildings and landing on our fire escape.

All of these wonders were performed in our back yard in a loving environment of our parents and other family members and friends as everyone in the neighborhood watched out for the children as they played.

A simple life that has been lost forever - never to be recaptured! Progress? Give me the good old days!

"Fences, Cardboard Boxes + Granma's Clothes line" - Brooklyn, N.Y.

Phil Brasso

TRYING TO GIVE GRANDMA'S CAT HER MEDICINE

Grandma's cat, an Angorra, was extremely intelligent and always knew that when we opened the cabinet door at a particular time that she was going to get her medicine and would find the most unusual hiding places. Grandma had a hard time catching her and when I was there she would always ask me to help her as she prayed that we wouldn't break anything.

WATCHING THE LOCAL GOSSIPERS
HAMILTON AVE. | BROOKLYN, NY 1943

In every neighborhood there are some ladies who have nothing to do, yet they are experts on every subject! Speaking among themselves they would say, "This woman does not know how to handle children! She lets them walk on the sidewalk without any shoes and they are only half dressed. She even lets them put their bare feet in filthy street puddles. She certainly does not know how to bring up children".

Christmas was a time for all the girls to display their talent in baking the most delicious cookies and pastries, which they would spend days preparing. This was a talent which the girls learned from an early age and their reward was seeing the joy it brought to the faces of family and friends as the holidays neared. These goodies were a real treat especially in the war years when sugar was rationed and very limited to each family.

AMAZED AT THE MERRY-GO-ROUND FELTON'S | CONEY ISLAND, 1945

What a magical place to be as a child in the post Depression years with all the bright lights and music as the horses galloped round and round in a circle. I would scream with glee as the carousel slowed down as I waited for my turn to climb into the saddle.

MANGIARE, MANGIARE, FACCIO GROSSA! (EAT, EAT, GET BIG)

Mothers and Grandmothers wanted us kids to eat and grow strong and healthy. Nothing seemed to please a mother as much as seeing her children enjoy the food which she had prepared.

FIREWORKS AND MUSIC AT ITALIAN FEAST
ST. STEPHEN'S CHURCH | BROOKLYN, NY 1940'S

Community life revolved around the church in the 1940's and a highlight of each neighborhood was The Feast of the Saints. Each family would set up a booth where they prepared their own specialty foods, such as peppers, onions and sausage, zapalas, and chestnuts, or "castagne" in Italian.

The Patron Saint would be paraded through the streets on the shoulders of "The Chosen" with the local priest or Monsignour leading the way. The women would rush to the front, where they were able to put their dollars into the bag carried by the priest so that everyone could see their generosity.

To this day, I cannot smell the wonderful smell of cooking peppers, onions and Italian sausage without memories of the Feast popping into my Head.

If you are planning a trip to New York in September you can experience the Feast of San Gennaro, New York City's longest-running, biggest and most revered religious outdoor festival in the United States.

19

CATCHING A FLY BALL IN CARROLL PARK | BROOKLYN, NY 1947

Carroll Park was a favorite playground for the neighborhood kids. Everyone was busy doing what ever they liked and of course, my favorite was catching the ball or anything else to do with baseball.

If you observe the neighborhood parks today, it's no wonder we face such a huge increase in obesity.

SAND IN THE PANTS

A day at the beach was a memorable experience with families flooding to the ocean to find relief from the heat, as air-conditioning was non-existent in the 1940's.

Families would spend the entire day at the beach and in the late afternoon as they prepared to leave they would always have to shake the sand from their bathing suits and suffer the pain of an extreme sunburn.

You can visit those same beaches today—which were completely covered with bathers in the 1940's—and you will see that there are very few people on the beach because they find their relief from home air-conditioning. A pleasure which has been lost to those who have never experienced just how refreshing it is to frolic in the Ocean when the sun is beating down to the point where it is almost unbearable.

DREAMING AND WISHING SOME DAY I'M GOING
TO BUY A BICYCLE | BROOKLYN, NY 1946

AT 74 YEARS OLD I GOT MY FIRST BICYCLE
A "HUFFY" MADE IN CHINA

COK-KA-RELLA, THE LOCAL BUM

Cok-ka-rella, the local bum saluting a stray dog "Heil Hitler"! Grandma chased him away with her broom.

Notice the V in the candy store window as my Uncle Tommy was coming home from the war.

TEACHING THE GIRLS HOW TO SEW

In the 1940's most of the women worked in the garment industry, better known as sweat shops and they taught their daughters how to sew at an early age. Some were interested and some were not! But they all had to learn.

14 GIRLS AND NO BOYS!

One of the neighborhood family's consisted of 14 girls and no boys and the father was so hungry for a boy that he often took advantage of a stray ball rolling into his small yard to capture the young man who threw it there. More than once I found myself squirming as he tried to show me the value of meeting a nice young girl. I wanted no part of that in those days.

Before air-conditioning and refrigerators with ice-makers, all ice was delivered by horse-drawn wagons. The men would unload large blocks of ice on the sidewalks. Then each family would come down from their apartments and he would fill their requests – "I'll take a quarter of a block" or half a block and so on.

I remember our family ordering a quarter block of ice for 25 cents. One man would chop the ice with an ice pick and the other man would place a burlap bag on his shoulder where he would place the ice and carry it two flights upstairs and place in our ice box.

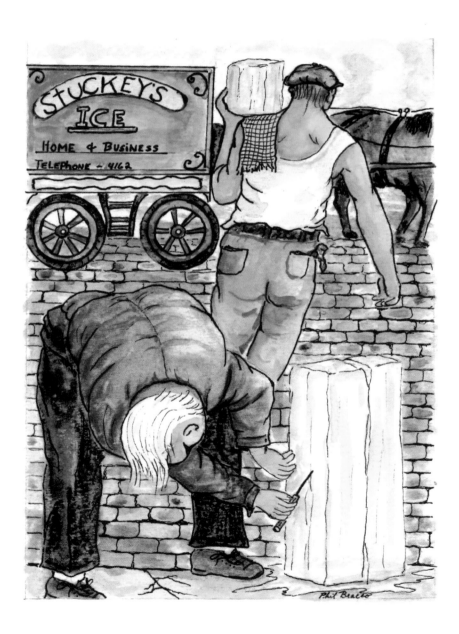

"Cooking Hot Mickeys (Potatoes) in a Empty Lot" - Brooklyn, N.Y. 1945

COOKING HOT MICKEYS (POTATOES) IN AN EMPTY LOT

When the summer months faded and the fresh clean autumn air arrived, neighborhood kids would go out into an old vacant lot and cook potatoes on a stick, over an open fire. Believe me, there were many old lots in the industrial area of "Red Hook".

Each kid had his own stick with a potato on the end. Each would take turns cooking their potato. If anyone had a sweet potato, that was the ultimate. Everyone had their own interpretation on how long it needed to cook. Usually the skin was jet black and so were our eyebrows! This was a result of standing too close to the open fire. Some bright kid said that his mother told him that eating the whole potato charred skin and all was very healthy. Every so often a hot ember from the fire would descend down on to our wool coats and of course set it afire. Those were the risks as we experienced the closest thing to camping out.

To this day, I still love to eat the skin of a baked potato as memories of fireflies dance in my head and I am once again transported back to those wonderful cool nights with the warmth of an open fire and the smell of potatoes baking, in the vacant lots of "Red Hook" Brooklyn.

HOME-MADE SCOOTERS

My Uncle Mike showed all the kids in the neighborhood how to make a scooter with old discarded metal roller skates. His popularity in the neighborhood was ended forever with the grown-ups!

It started with one, then two, and soon all the kids in the neighborhood had scooters. There we came, kid after kid, riding those scooters with the noise of metal roller skates grinding on the concrete sidewalks. The noise was very irritating to the ears of the adult's and was even worse when every dog on the block started barking and running down the street with us. People were shouting, "Go play around the block!"

The very old Italian people kept yelling and screaming words in their native tongue – I'm sure they were complimentary and not many bad words!

Dogs from way off in the distance picked up on those dogs barking and they too joined in on the symphony.

HIDING ON MY MOTHER AT MACY'S

My favorite game was to hide from my Mother at every Department Store she visited. The best hiding place was in between the racks of Ladies Dresses. After her endless screams went unanswered she would go into panic mode. I loved Macy's because there were so many places to hide.

When it looked like I might be exposed or caught I would run downstairs to the bargain basement where it would sometimes take hours for her to find me. Going shopping for my Mother was a nightmare since there were no baby sitters to leave me with.

When we arrived home, my Father was informed of my daily activities. The end result was handled by my Father in his usual way – another backside warming!

SHEETS AND PILLOW CASES

There appeared on a weekly basis a large Jewish woman who carried a large bedspread filled with table cloths, sheets and pillow cases which she carried on her head. She would go door to door selling these items to all the local families. She would take the bundle off her head and untie the bundle and display her linens.

In our case she would carry her bundle up two flights of stairs. If you were a regular customer, she would often say, "Give me 25 cents or whatever and I'll return next week for the rest." This was before Wal-Mart and mail order.

SNAKE VENDOR AT THE ITALIAN FEAST ENTERTAINS THE CHILDREN

Every Italian Feast had a vendor selling balloons, whirls and snakes. I don't know why, but colorful snakes on a string were very popular. The first time I saw them I ran from the vendor. To be safe, when asked, I always took the balloon instead of the snake. My sisters always took the colorful whirls. After hours of playing with my balloon I would release it and observe it flying into the night sky, high above all the festivities.

While my parents vowed never to buy me a balloon ever again, I was fascinated as it vanished into the darkness.

SWINGING ON THE FRONT GATE

Don't ask me what the attraction was to swing on Grandma's front gate. We were warned repeatedly about using the front gate as a swing but like all kids, if no one is around, we took our turns swinging back and forth. This worked out pretty good until our uncle came home from work and warmed our backsides. The swinging stopped immediately but was again back in action after my uncle disappeared and one of us kids was on the lookout.

WASHING THE STREETS

During the summer months the department of sanitation would send a water truck down our street and spray the gutters which would wash all the dirt down the street and into the sewer system. Next the street cleaners would sweep the gutters clean and they would pick up the garbage with shovels and deposit it into a large barrel which had wheels and they would move along.

Next came the fire department, which would open up the fire hydrants and check the water pressure. When this happened, all the neighbors and their kids would take off most of their clothes and wet their feet in the flow of water coming down the street.

There was always one kid with a pan or a small barrel that they would fill up with water and stay in. Some kids made paper boats which they inserted in the water and ran down the street as it finally disappeared into the sewer. Yes –All the kids got washed as well as the gutters!

MIDGET MOBSTER

In our neighborhood there were a bunch of local gamblers, crooks and hoodlums which included a local midget that ran all kinds of illegal operations
right in front of the local police station which was only a half block away from our home. We would watch in amazement as he was frequently hauled down to the jail for reasons unknown to us.

ORGAN GRINDER AND FORTUNE TELLER

For one penny, a parrot would pick out your fortune from a card box and place it in the cup while the organ grinder played music to amuse us.

All the neighborhood kids would run as soon as they heard the music and laugh like crazy as each person read their fortune.

Later in life, I discovered that the music was the Italian National Anthem.

CHOCOLATE EGG CREAMS AT SERGIE'S

Sergie's, a local candy store on the corner of 1st Place and Court Street was a favorite for the Chocolate Egg Cream as well as an Orzata drink which is made from an Almond Syrup and Seltzer. If you would like to try this favorite drink from my childhood, you can still purchase Orzata Syrup and just mix it with Seltzer Water over ice.

Chocolate marshmallow and jelly candy and long pretzel sticks were a must to dunk in our drinks.

We always felt welcome at Sergie's because the owner, Pete Sergie knew every kid in the neighborhood by name.

CHANGING CLOTHES IN FRONT OF 3 MILLION PEOPLE UNDER MOTHER'S BED SPREAD | CONEY ISLAND 1946

People ran to the beach to seek relief from the hot summer days and lacking the money to pay for a bathhouse many kids simply wrapped themselves in their Mother's bedspread to change into and out of their bathing suit.

While a friend held the bedspread around us we struggled to get out of our wet suit when suddenly the friend would drop the spread and cause us to sink down to the sand in search of cover and of course the chore of removing the scratchy sand from our suit would begin once again as all the other kids howled with laughter.

GETTING A LECTURE ON HOW TO THROW SNOWBALLS

During our frequent snowball fights we would run and jump and dive in to order to avoid a fast flying snowball headed in our direction. In order to survive the fight it required a system so I would make up a huge pile of snowballs prior to the fight. I was throwing the snowballs as quick as I could when all of a sudden Mrs. Bernardi appeared just as my snowball reached the spot where she was walking. All of my friends thought for sure I was going to be reprimanded and broke out in laughter as I quickly apologized and Mrs. Bernardi politely told me how to throw a snowball safely.

She added that if I wanted to be a good ball player that I needed to improve on my accuracy and, "When I come home from work in the future I expect to see some improvement!" She bid me goodbye and then proceeded to make her way home through the snow as though nothing had ever happened.

I GOT THE SAME REACTION EVERY TIME

I always got the same reaction from my Dad or my Uncles if I did something wrong. In anger, they would put their hand in their mouth and bite down with their teeth.

In Italian they would either whisper or shout, "Buza-in-ah-cheez" or "I think I will kill you." This was usually accompanied by a severe beating and in extremely rare cases a leather belt would finalize a good shellacking, as it was called in those days.

I must admit they showed total compassion since they didn't ever hit me with the metal belt buckle.

41

SWINGING AND CLIMBING IN CARROLL PARK

As kids, we spent many hours and days playing in Carroll Park. Climbing, swinging and jumping. Hanging upside down was the ultimate. We would swing like monkeys, one hand after the other.

Sometimes we would just sit on top and watch the world go by. It was always shady under the beautiful old shade trees in the park and offered us relief from the heat in the summer.

Sometimes in the late afternoon the men would play softball and we were amazed that they smacked the softballs clear over the park and into the brownstone buildings across the street. We had favorite hero players who all had nicknames such as King Kong, Superman, Mahogany, Mosquito and other various names. Life was carefree but beautiful for us kids — as we really knew nothing about the hard times of that decade.

GETTING A PADDLING PLAYING A GAME CALLED "HOT BEANS"

One of the favorite street games called "Hot Beans" brought out all the boys in the neighborhood because they always had the chance to relieve their frustrations by chasing other boys and whacking them with a paddle. Some reached the safety of the den without getting whacked!

Winters first snow saw us head for Prospect Park where we all shared my cousin Louie's sled since only rich kids owned their own. The biggest thrill was to roll off the sled before it slammed into a tree.

Each of us enjoyed rolling off into the soft snow. One day the sleigh ride ended abruptly since my cousin Georgie waited a little too long to roll off and slammed head on into a tree. Our Sleigh ride ended early that day but the next day found us back at it again.

AGGRAVATING JOE THE PIZZA MAN

My cousin Sal taught me how to stand by Joe's Pizza store on Hamilton Avenue and just stare at the people enjoying their pizza. These stares brought on a reaction of pity from the customers and many times they would offer us a slice of their pizza. This practice was used so much and Joe would become agitated each time we appeared and stared from the window into the pizzeria at his customers.

One evening I guess his nerves got the best of him as he grabbed a large knife and chased us half way down the street to scare us away. We really got the message this time! No more staring into Joe's Pizza store window although years later my wife and I made it a habit to eat Joe's Pizza at least once a week for as long as Joe lived. I can still see Joe and his wife and 2 daughters as they fed the wood fired brick oven where his pizza could never be duplicated after his death. Even though his daughters had a professional life when they were grown they still came back to try and keep the pizzeria going when their father became ill. It was family pride.

OH NO I'M NEXT - AUNT KISSING TIME

In Italian families, kids had to kiss their aunts every time they came to visit and boy did we have a lot of aunts! They seemed to come from every section of Brooklyn. I hated to kiss them because they smelled of cheap "Toilet Water", thick make-up, red rouge and wet sloppy kisses which would leave a thick impression of lipstick on my face. Sometimes I got more than one kiss. In my eyes as a youngster they seemed to be like gigantic monsters waiting to crush me in their large fatty arms.

POLLY NOSES IN CAROLL PARK | BROOKLYN, 1948

Sandwiched between Court Street and Smith Street and between President and Carroll Street is a small area called "Carroll Park".

At a certain time of the year some of the trees would drop small pods to the ground. The kids gathered the pods and cut them in half and placed them on their noses. They were called poly noses. All of the kids walked around the park with these green pods stuck to their noses. The older people who sat in the park looked at us in total despair. What will become of these kids with such fantasies? Imagination was a wonderful thing in those post depression years as children found amusement in some of the simplest things.

I'M ABOUT TO GET A PIZA-GEEL KISS" (I HAVE NO IDEA WHAT IT MEANS)

Getting a "piza-geel kiss" was half torture and it was administered in the following way:

The kisser was usually an aunt or grandmother who would grab your cheeks tightly with both hands and squeezing while pushing your lips close to theirs. Next, they would kiss you on the lips and this was accompanied with a loud shout, "Che bella raggazzo!," or "What a beautiful boy," in English.

Why they call it a "pizza-geel kiss," I'll never know. My cheeks remained red and sore for several hours.

Author's Note: Modern kids do not have to endure such punishment and they really have no idea what they have missed. My three sons, Jack, Sal and Scott remember them well however.

TAKEOFF YOUR SHOES AND COOL YOUR FEET

The summer heat in New York was unbearable and living in Brooklyn was no exception. We kids were always on the lookout for the Department of sanitation inspector who would open up the fire hydrants to make sure they were operating correctly.

Sometimes the adults, seeking relief from the heat, would open up the Johnny Pumps just so the kids could play in the cool water and refresh themselves. When this would happen all the kids would take off their shoes and stomp in the cool water. Ladies would wet their handkerchiefs and place them over their necks or wipe their brows to cool off. The cool water hitting the hot streets created a steamy vapor of which the smell remains cemented in my memory still.

I can still feel the cool water hitting my warm feet and toes. Wiggling my toes was as pleasant as stomping or jumping about in the cool water as it rushed down the street with a trail of kids chasing it for the last moments of relief until the next time.

**MOM'S FRIEND JOSIE GETTING CAR SICK ON
DAD'S NEW CAR | ENTRANCE TO THE GEORGE
WASHINGTON BRIDGE**

An auto trip out of the city was an excitement to be shared
with others and on this day my Mother invited her good
friend Josie to come along with our family as we headed for
the countryside however as we approached the entrance
to the George Washington Bridge she experienced car
sickness and to the chagrin of the rest of us, especially my
little brother who had a very weak tolerance for anything,
turned yellow. Well, needless to say, my father turned the
car around and rushed back to Brooklyn and a place to
wash his brand new Nash Rambler. Another one of the
great family Sunday afternoon drives.

UPON SEEING A ZEPPELIN FOR THE FIRST TIME

While playing in our backyard, we kids were startled when we saw a zeppelin for the first time. Every kid was pointing to the sky. We had no idea what it was. It was very exciting and mysterious as it slowly moved into the summer sky. The old Italian men had their own thoughts about it. Some thought it was spies. Others said the government was looking for Germans in the area and of course there was one old man who would say that the Italian Marconi invented the Zeppelin. To him, Marconi invented almost everything. As kids, we were so gullible. In today's world this sighting would be compared to seeing a UFO.

"WORKERS PLACING THEIR BETS WITH CAMELLA THE BOOKIE"

WORKERS PLACING THEIR BETS WITH CAMELLA THE BOOKIE

Just 3 houses away from the 76th precinct police station workers found a way to place their bets with Camella the bookie. She used her clothesline to exchange money and numbers in full view of the entire neighborhood. The police were completely oblivious to the interaction between the players and the bookie.

When we played in our yard we could see dollar bills on the clothes line going back and forth. I asked my Grandma, "Why is there money on the clothesline?" Her answer was, "Camella's money got wet and she is drying it out" which seemed sensible to me at the time. So we went back to digging holes in the backyard and playing once again.

Just above the fence next to my Grandfather, in his backyard is where the money was exchanged using the clothesline.

THE BALDY BEAN KIDS OF BROOKLYN

On a dare from my friend Marco, a bunch of us boys went to the barber and got a "Baldy Bean" haircut and left the shop with evidence of past cuts and knocks on the head as we all had some form of various scars.

Dressed in our new baseball uniforms we found great pleasure in tipping our hats to the ladies as we passed by their stoop and to watch as they gasped at how we looked. As we passed they yelled, "Bazza, Bazza," and chased us away with their brooms!

CRYING FOR A HOT DOG | SMITH & FULTON ST. | 1940'S

On occasion, my mother would take me shopping on Fulton Street. There was a great hot dog stand on the corner of Smith and Fulton. I would keep a sharp eye on the stand as we approached it. I would go into convulsions crying for a hot dog. My pleas started with "I'm starving, I can't walk anymore, I'm too weak" and my pleas ended by lying down on the sidewalk. My mother would scream for me to get up before someone stepped on me.

I knew from experience that if I were to delay our journey in front of the hot dog stand, that the smell and aroma of hot dogs would get to her. Mother loved hot dogs, especially Sabrett. By delaying our shopping, the aromas had a chance to enter her nostrils and excite her taste buds. Finally she would call out to the vendor, "Two hot dogs with mustard and sauerkraut and two Cokes please.

This technique never failed me and even into my adult life anytime I was out with my mother we would always have to stop for a hot dog the minute she spotted the stand.

THE FIRST BRACCO ON TV

I was selected to appear on the Happy Felton Show after winning the baseball talent competition.

My father, along with his co-workers at the Brooklyn Army base delayed their lunch hour and crowded into the nearest local bar to watch the event.

JUMPING FROM 2ND STORY INTO THE POOL
RUSSELLO'S HOUSE | 3RD ST., BROOKLYN

My friend Nick Russello had one of the first above-ground pools in the neighborhood that took up the entire back yard with not an inch to spare.

Needless to say his house became a favorite hangout for us boys as we would climb to the second story and jump out the window into the refreshing pool as his mother watched nervously from the ground floor.

WE LOOKED SO RAGGY THAT THE TUG BOAT SAILORS GAVE US FRUIT AND SANDWICHES

During the early years of the 1940's, my cousin Sal and I would roam the waterfronts of Brooklyn. We got to know every street in Red Hook and we would play on the barges which were docked along the waterfront.

We became good friends with the Captain's and sailor's who worked on the ships and tugboats.

Seeing us with patched clothing, the men would toss us some fruit or sandwiches whenever we showed up at the dock. We loved to hear them blow the horn and when they saw us they would give it an extra pull.

THE SOUND OF HORESHOES CLANGING AND CLAPPING ON COBBLESTONE STREETS

The sound of metal horseshoes clanking down the street was an invitation to the neighborhood women to come and shop for fresh vegetables. After all these years the sound of the metal horse shoes clanking on the cobblestone as women appeared on the stoop with their baskets to buy fresh food for the evening meal is still vivid in my memory. The vendor would sing out what he was selling as he approached the group of waiting women and could be heard from one end of the street to the other. Soon the many smells of fresh cooking vegetables would fill the air.

COK-KA-RELLA, THE LOCAL BUM

Cok-Ka-Rella was the local neighborhood drunk that could be found sleeping in the morning by someone's store front, or snoozing away in the park.

Even though he was drunk and homeless, he would share coins from his pocket with the kids who approached him. An early lesson I learned to be able to see good in people where we might least expect it.

NEVER QUITE ABLE TO FILL HIS SHOES

During the depression and for several years after the men had a tough time providing for their families. No matter how hard it was my Dad always managed to provide healthy food and occasional treats for 5 children as he struggled with earning a regular income. I would continually try to wear his shoes.

Phil Bracco

A JELLY APPLE AND CHARLOTTE ROUSSE

One of the rare treats for my sister and I as we enjoyed a
jelly apple or a Charlotte Rousse. We learned to appreciate
things after waiting for so long to get them.

**ME ON DAD'S BACK, CEREMONY AT CITY HALL
(BOROUGH HALL), CHEERING OUR BELOVED DODGERS**

During those lean years everyone needed a hero and the Brooklyn Dodgers was ours.

The winning of the 1941 National League Pennant was a reason for the entire neighborhood to celebrate. The whole neighborhood rushed to Borough Hall to see their hero's as confetti filled the sky from the windows of all the surrounding buildings. It was a time for celebration!

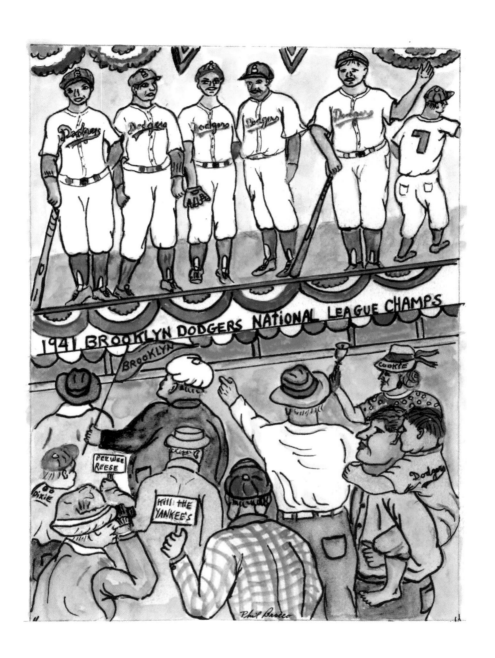

66

DEFONTE'S SANDWICH SHOP TODAY

EATING LUNCH WITH THE WORKING MEN

There was no place on earth that could compare with having lunch on the sidewalks of Brooklyn by Nick DeFonte's Sandwich Shop on Columbia Street. I loved to get there at noon because the shop would be packed with Industrial, Factory and Dock workers as well as Teachers, Lawyers and other professional people. The counter was about 15 feet long with people three-deep, screaming out the sandwiches they wanted such as: shrimp with calamari sauce, Italian cold cuts, pepper and eggs, pepper and sausages, and an array of just about anything your mind could conjure up in Italian foods. Our favorite drink was a Manhattan Special, which happened to be bottled in Brooklyn on Manhattan Avenue.

The sandwich was made up in less than a minute and you had better yell out your selection quickly because it would be in a brown bag ready to go by the time you got the words out of your mouth.

In all my life I have never experienced such an operation anywhere else and I probably never will.

I still cannot come up with a reason why these sandwiches taste better sitting on a street curb with pigeons walking around eating up the crumbs.

Even today, a trip to New York always includes a trip back to Columbia Street and a sandwich from Nick's. A lone building surrounded by all vacant stores but still able to lure the crowds of surrounding industrial and business areas.

WAIT UP, I'M PUTTING CARDBOARD IN MY SHOES

Money was scarce in those days and a hole in our shoes was no reason to dispose of them. Many times I have searched for cardboard to use as an innersole and then they were good for a few more months.

Something our kids of today can only imagine in this "Throw Away Society".

SATURDAY MORNING SHOPPING ON UNION STREET AND COLUMBIA

Before the days of super markets the people of our neighborhood shopped on Union Street. From Columbia to Hicks Street vendors were lined up on both sides of the street. They had everything from makeshift wagons, pushcarts, horse driven wagons and any kind of structure where they could display their goods.

Every Saturday my Mother and Grandmother would take large shopping bags and proceed up one side of the street and down the other. Everything was fresh- freshly harvested vegetables, fresh baked bread, a pork store with many different cuts of pork and homemade sausages, fresh mozzarella, fresh ricotta, olives of all kinds and every other kind of food stuff imaginable.

Vendors were hawking their wares and women were trying to get things cheaper while kids ran and played and dogs barked with car horns blowing for people to move out of the way.

All of your food needs for the week could be purchased within these couple of blocks along Union Street. From our home on Hamilton Avenue it was like walking down Broadway. There were Mattress stores, dry goods stores, five and dime stores, a movie theatre, pastry shops, hardware stores where anything one needed could be found here.

The most amazing part was that not only did the vendor know the adults by name but also their children. As you approached he would already know what you wanted and how you wanted it prepared. If a mother was unable to shop for some reason she could send her child with complete confidence that she would get exactly what she wanted.

I often wonder, have we really progressed in this modern world where even your neighbor often does not know your name.

ANNUAL HALLOWEEN FLOUR FIGHTS I FORGOT TO DUCK

At Halloween, we knew nothing about trick or treat but a neighborhood tradition was to get a pair of our Dad's socks and go to Sessa's bakery where they would fill the socks with flour and then the fun would begin. We would romp the sidewalks swinging our flour filled socks and if you weren't quick you just might end up with a black eye. By the time it got good and dark our neighborhood looked like a haunted village with everything covered with chalk and flour.

The adults would walk for blocks just to avoid the chance of getting fit by a fast flying sock.

With the announcement of D-Day, people celebrated with hopes of finally seeing their sons and daughters return home from the war. At last, victory was in sight.

COME HERE "YAP-PA-EEL"

A couple of houses down from us lived an old man who must have had Alzheimer disease or something similar and he could hardly move. Each summer morning his family would sit him outside with a table and chair so he could get fresh air and watch the neighborhood activity.

On the table sat a 5 gallon carboy of red wine and a bird cage holding a parrot. The parrot would repeat everything the old man would say and since they both spoke Italian, I was unable to understand much of what they were saying. He would sit there with his old dog next to his feet smoking a corn cob pipe as he frequently spit into a spittoon on the sidewalk.

My Uncle Mike made me a small little scooter which I would ride for hours up and down the sidewalk where he was sitting. Each time I passed he would mumble curse words in Italian which was repeated by his parrot. If I stopped to listen, so I could understand what he was saying he would gesture with his fingers for me to come closer to him. I didn't trust him at all and I always kept my distance from him and his parrot. He would call to me, "Vinay ca yap pa eel," and the parrot would immediately take up the chant of "Yap pa eel, yap pa eel, yap pa eel" over and over and over.

Years later I found out that the meaning of "Yap pa eel" was a little hot caper.

My uncle Sammy owned the Court Street Pastry Shop and he asked my cousin Louie and I to find him a cat to keep the mice away. We found a small fragile white kitten at Carroll Street and Court Street and took it to him. He was so delighted that he gave us a lemon ice and an Italian cookie for our efforts.

About six to eight months passed when my sister and I visited his pastry shop. While we were talking, out from the back room came a huge ugly looking creature. My sister got scared and ran outside. I had no idea what kind of an animal it was. It had a round solid body like a dog and a fat ugly face with chubby legs and it wobbled from side to side as it walked.

I was a little nervous at first since I had never seen anything like it and I asked "What is that?". Uncle Sammy replied that it was the little kitten we had brought him several months ago. When I asked, "What happened to it?" he replied that the cat sat at the back of the shop and ate all of the discarded Cannolli Cream. Be careful when you go to an Italian bakery because this just might happen to you!

BUYING SHOES TWO SIZES LARGER

Just before school started my Mother would take me to buy a new pair of shoes. When the salesman brought out a size chart my Mother said she did not need it because she always bought the shoes two sizes to big so they would last until the end of the school year.

It never bothered me that the shoes were too big as long as I got the free pencil set that came with each pair of new shoes.

YES, THAT'S ME GETTING ANOTHER BEATING OVER THE THIEF OF BAGHDAD MOVIE

When the "Thief of Baghdad" came to our neighborhood theatre, my grandmother gave me the money to go see it.

What happened on this day probably had an effect on my outlook for the rest of my life. I was engulfed into a world of adventure, imagination and a spirit of freedom. As Sinbad rode his magic carpet over Baghdad, my imagination brought the scene to life as I watched him uncork the small bottle lying on the beach and the Genie came out. The Genie flying along in the air with Sabu holding onto his hair as they both flew to the kingdom in the sky. The mechanical flying horses accompanied them back to the palace.

I was so engrossed into the on screen fantasy and I stayed and watched the show over and over again, completely forgetting the time. As Darkness approached and I had not returned home the whole family was out looking for me.

My Grandmother told my father that she had given me the money to see the show and he entered into the Happy Hour Theatre to look for me and there I sat, still gazing at the screen. He dragged me from the theatre and took off his belt and hit me all the way home to Hamilton Avenue. He was so happy to see me he could not contain himself.

"YES THAT'S ME GETTING ANOTHER BEATING OVER THE THIEF OF BAGDAD MOVIE"

TIME, DATE, YEAR - 8 PM DEC. 24, 1942

During the depression years, money was scarce and a Christmas tree was a luxury, but my Dad took me out after 6 PM on December 24th to find a tree for our family.

All the Christmas Tree Vendors had abandoned their stands by then leaving behind all of the unsold trees where we selected one and returned home to where my Mother would bring out homemade ornaments along with some home-baked cookies and we would all have a wonderful night decorating the tree with no knowledge of the hardship my parents faced.

ELECTION NIGHT BONFIRES - A BROOKLYN TRADITION

Election Night in our neighborhood was an event enjoyed by kids and adults alike. Each year, as Election Night drew near, every boy in the neighborhood began collecting wood, boxes, bushels, cellar doors, old wooden newsstands, and wine crates. Every Italian in our neighborhood made wine, so we had an ample supply of boxes. Most of the wine makers stored the empty crates in their basement for this special event. When the word was given, us boys would clean out their basements and cellars and all the wood was placed in the middle of the street in one large pile.

We had spotters on the rooftop watching out for the fire department. The fire department would patrol the streets to put out any fires that were started. Our strategy was to start our fires at 10PM. By this time, the activities throughout Brooklyn would have settled down and the fire department would be at ease thinking that all the fires were over.

Finally, the go ahead word was given and gasoline was spread onto the wood and the pile was ignited. Flames reached high into the night sky and you could hear the crowd shouting ooh's and ahh's. Soon we would hear the sirens off in the distance coming to extinguish our bon fire. When they arrived, with the first spray of water would come the boo's from everyone in the neighborhood.

I really think that the adults enjoyed this tradition more than us kids. No longer can you see the bonfires of Election Night, as they dissipated into the air with the ashes forever.

MY FIRST TOOTH EXTRACTION - I'M ABOUT TO GET SLAMMED

In those days we never had to worry about a dentist because Grandpa always knew how to take care of pulling a tooth.

BOO-NA-GEEL, A KID'S BEST FRIEND

Boo-na-geel was the only name I ever knew him by. He always came to my defense when I got into trouble in the neighborhood. He would tell the old Italian ladies who were badgering me to "Go home and cook for your husband!"

**MY UNCLE JOHN'S WEDDING -
I REFUSED TO WALK DOWN THE AISLE**

For months on end the ladies in the family were planning a super wedding which was to take place in Jersey City, New Jersey. I had no idea what they were planning. Weeks before the wedding they took me to be fitted for a tuxedo complete with a pair of black patent leather shoes. They would tell me almost every day how I should walk down the aisle as the ring bearer.

Then came the ill-fated day when they took me to church for the ceremony. From the other side of the church appeared a short fat ugly little girl. She had flowers around her head, ladies earrings on and a basket full of flowers wearing what to me was a really ugly dress. To me she looked like a little witch. Everyone was telling me to look how pretty she was and all I had to do was to hold her hand and walk down the aisle. I took another look at her and there was no way I was going to walk down the aisle with her.

They all wanted to kill me because it was getting close to time for the bride to arrive. I knew that if I lived through that day that I would live to a ripe old age.

My father was the only one smiling since he did not want to go in the first place.

82

MY AUNTS UPON SEEING A MOUSE (OR A "ZUCCULA" IN ITALIAN)

My aunts could run their mouths off with the best of them and would fight anyone at the drop of a hat or if one word was said that they didn't like.

But to my amazement, a little field mouse came by one day in our backyard. What happened next was something I will never forget. The mouse ran by and screeched while each of them ran in total panic screaming as they went.

My two cousins and I looked up and found our aunt's standing on three picnic tables holding their dresses up over their heads while screaming at the top of their lungs. My Grandmother was yelling at them "SCIATTONE!" in Italian, which is like "slob" in English. "Your underwear is showing! Pull your dresses down."

Each of them were shaking violently as my Grandmother shook her head as she mumbled in Italian, calling them "The brave ones!"

THE NIGHT BRUNO'S OIL CO. SAVED OUR FAMILY FROM FREEZING TO DEATH | 1942, BROOKLYN

The winters were brutal for the families along Hamilton Avenue during a storm. One such evening, our family gathered around a small oil burning stove for warmth. We all knew that the amount of oil left in the stove was running low and would not last much longer. We were bundled in blankets and any other conceivable wrap in an attempt to stay warm as we huddled there next to the stove. The doors and windows were stuffed with newspapers and old rags in an attempt to keep the cold winter wind out.

My Father decided to go out and try to find a place to get more fuel so he took me and a 5 gallon can and we headed out into the bitter cold. The visibility was poor and nothing but snow drifts and the sound of wind screaming through the cold air kept us focused.

After searching several streets, looking in both directions, we encountered a man carrying a 5 gallon can full of fuel. He told us that the Bruno Oil Company was making their final delivery for the evening and that it was parked at the Hamilton Avenue Ferry. After much effort we finally found the Bruno Truck, pumping oil into the tanks at a commercial building. My Father begged the driver to sell us just 5 gallons of fuel to prevent his family from freezing. The driver was very compassionate and said that the building would not miss 5 gallons of kerosene as he filled our can.

We arrived back home just as the stove was running out of fuel so I guess you can say that the Bruno Truck Driver saved our lives on that fateful cold night in the winter of 1942.

WATCH OUT, HERE THEY COME AGAIN

During my youth we would visit my Grandparents in Jersey City, New Jersey. It really was quite a trip to get there from Brooklyn. We would take the subway to New York City and then transfer to the Hudson Tubes which ran under the Hudson River to Hoboken. From there we would take a trolley to Central Avenue in Jersey City. The terminal seemed extremely large from a child's view. It looked like a bee hive with trolleys coming and going and lots of commotion.

While waiting for our trolley, I would look up at the steel rafters above our heads where hundreds of pigeons were flying around in all directions. Some were just sitting there perched on a rafter, while others were walking around on the ground with their familiar strut as though they owned the terminal.

When we arrived at my Grandparents house I told my Grandfather about all of the pigeons flying above our heads at the terminal. Not realizing at the time, what an impression it would make on my young mind he said "The pigeons sit there just waiting to do poop on your head. And many of them will dive down so that they get a better aim at your head and body." This was probably the worst thing he could have said to me as he spoke in his familiar language of Italian. Upon entering the terminal on our next trip, I began running and screaming in Italian, "paloma-va-a-gogga-copa-a-gabba." I would be yelling, "Here they come again as I ducked to try and miss getting hit on the head as I screamed "Watch out lady, he is pooping on your head!"

My actions caused nervousness with the people on the platform and they began jumping from one side to the other pulling their children with them as the birds flew above their heads. My Mother tried desperately to stop me but to no avail. Before long everyone in the terminal was looking up with some trying to cover their heads with their purses or pocketbooks. The birds were winning. Almost every person at the terminal received a bird blessing. Most of the people had no idea what my mother was shouting in Italian and of course I was repeating it in English.

When someone got hit I would scream with laughter as my Mother hit me with her purse. Her cries went on deaf ears as she kept repeating, "Stop! You are scaring the American people."

Finally the trolley came in and we boarded and settled into our seats. I was quick to point out how many spots were on my mother's hat and dress. This made her angry and in order to take revenge on me she would twist my ears, thus ending the experience of the pigeons going poop on our heads.

RICE, CONFETTI AND FLOWER PETALS FOR THE NEWLY WEDS

An Italian neighborhood tradition was when someone in the neighborhood got married the wedding procession would tour the Bride and Groom's streets with special instructions to stop at each of their homes. Neighbors and children would be lined up to throw rice at the couple as the car stopped in front of their house. The elderly ladies, with trays in their hands, each containing rice, confetti, candied sugar coated almonds from the pastry shop, flower petals and loose coins converged on the bridal car as they passed the tray to the newlyweds. I never knew the significance of this tradition but I guess it was a gesture of good luck.

Usually, on Saturday afternoon around 4PM a wedding took place and the entire neighborhood would rush to the church to watch the wedding procession. Most of the time they had no idea who was getting married and it really did not make any difference as in those days a wedding was a very joyous occasion as well as one of the sacraments and they wished them a good marriage.

The rapid sound of the church bells signaled the news that a wedding was about to take place. But if the bells rang slowly it meant there was a funeral so everyone was elated to hear the bells ring fast and long.

There was no way anyone could get married without the entire neighborhood knowing about it. A tradition long lost as we watch the decline in marriages in today's society.

MRS. DONAVAN RULED WITH A WOOD STICK

Here's one for the books! My first day in class, Mrs. Donovan would walk up and down the aisles with her wooden pointed stick which created fear in all of her students. I was sitting in the second seat of the first row next to some storage closets when she called me up to the closet. Then she opened the door and pointed to a picture of a man taped to the door of a magazine with a man in a Hollywood costume. She asked me if I knew this man. Upon looking at it I said, "Yes! That's my father." She then pointed out to me that he sat at a certain desk in her classroom and that she watched him grow into an adult and later a movie actor in the silent movies.

She then rattled off the names of every Bracco in my family that she personally taught. My father, my Uncles Ralph, Mike, and Tommy, as well as my Aunts , Suzie, Aggie, Betty and Katie, and now she was teaching my sisters, Bridget and Terry, and me.

She must have been teaching from around 1910 thru 1945 at least. A strong feeling of belonging was cemented into our very being as the ghosts of family members walked the halls with us and their names glared out at us from all the textbooks.

She was very tough, but everyone had to learn regardless of what their I.Q. was. It amazed me how alert she was and not a mosquito could go by without her knowing about it.

My cousins Louie and Georgie were fortunate in that their parents had gotten them roller skates however my Father was fearful of what might happen if I had skates. When I finally got skates my cousins took me to Prospect Park to teach me how to use them. After several hours and many falls to the concrete later, it was time to head for home. Having spent our carfare on ice cream, we decided to skate home.

They pointed me down West 9th Street towards Red Hook which is a continuous decline downhill and in the process I hit parked cars, knocked over a lady carrying her groceries and my ice cream ended up all over a parked automobile. Heaven only knows why I was not killed since I went through several avenues with cars going in both directions.

By the time I got home, I looked like I had been in either a war or a fight with bruises and blood on several parts of my body. My cousins thought it was funny that I lost control of my balance so many times before we got to Second Place and Court Street and familiar flat territory.

Several years later, I became so good at skating that the Brooklyn Red Devils offered me a skating contract at the age of 17. Like a few other opportunities, my Father ran them off.

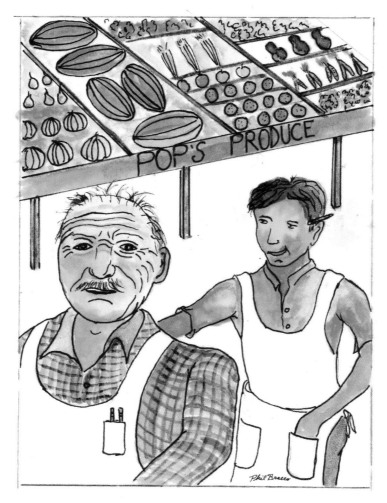

GRANDPA STARING INTO SPACE | WAIT TIL' I GET MY WIFE AT HOME

My Grandfather had a fruit and vegetable stand in Jersey City, New Jersey. My Grandmother came up with a brilliant idea that I could go help him for a few weeks during the summer months. She gave me a white apron and a sharp pencil for my ear and I really thought I was a big fruit and vegetable man then.

I was delivered to his stand, by my Uncle Johnny who immediately took off so he would not have to witness the catastrophe which was about to happen. When my Grandfather, Frank Saverese, saw me standing there in front of his stand with my white apron on was completely overcome with emotions and joy! His face turned blood red and he was speechless for a good hour. He would walk around shaking his head while looking up at the sky. I knew he was thanking God for his new help. He kept mumbling something in Italian about his wife.

Next he went to the back of the store and sat on an orange crate with his hands folded as if he was praying. I could not believe how impressed he was to have me come all the way from Brooklyn to help him. My Fruit and Vegetable experience lasted less than two days. I was shipped back to Brooklyn with a $20 bill in my pocket. I was truly blessed by having a Grandfather who loved me so much.

MOTHER WORRYING OVER A SICK CHILD

An expression of concern could be seen on the faces of most women during those hard times of the depression years and their only enjoyment was in the warmth of their family as they thanked God everyday for sparing their loved ones from even greater hardships – that of the loss of a family member as they prayed for the end to this dreadful war.

TOTALLY FASCINATED BY HORN AND HARDART RESTAURANTS

Going to Horn and Hardart Automat was a real treat for us. I could not believe how you could hand the cashier a dollar bill and he would place his hand in a bucket of nickels and with one hand deliver onto a marble tray exactly one dollar in nickels. I could never figure out how he did it but I guess from years of experience he could feel the exact weight of 20 nickels.

I enjoyed placing a nickel in the chocolate milk dispenser and out of the silver lions' mouth came exactly one glass of hot chocolate milk.

Chocolate cupcakes were one of my favorites and it required two nickels and with the twist of a knob a little window would open and I would reach in for my chocolate cupcakes. I was fascinated with all the little windows which contained all sorts of foods and desserts. I tried to look inside the tiny windows to see how it worked. Behind the scenes sheltered from the public were workers who replenished the items as they were sold.

The wholesome goodness of the fresh food served is still vivid in my memory as we have moved on to the fast foods of today which can in no way compare to the goodness of Horn and Hardart.

What a wonderful experience it was and I wish we could take a trip back in time to experience it once more.

During the late 40's and early 50's, the United States was inflicted with the disease known as Polio. In almost every city the scare became epidemic in proportion. People everywhere were searching for any medicine or remedy which might ward off this dreaded disease. Our neighborhood was no exception. Every family would look to the elders for advice and guidance. How their knowledge came about I will never know.

They said that camphor would keep Polio away from the children so every neighborhood kid had camphor stuffed in their pockets. Ladies made camphor necklaces, bracelets and in some cases would wash their children with camphor before sending them off to school. We smelled like hell and the teachers had no idea why all of these Italian kids smelled like camphor. It got so bad that all the other children stayed away from us while holding their noses.

Teachers wrote notes to all the parents in the neighborhood but to no avail. Eventually the Salk Vaccine came out and saved us from the fear of the dreaded disease of Polio. The elders were proud of their remedy since no child in our neighborhood got Polio.

PHIL THE FISHMAN WOULD ALWAYS BUY ME AN ICE CREAM

Every Friday, you could set your watch to it, the cries of Phil the fish man could be heard off in the distance. His voice could be heard above any distracting city noises. His calls for fish were very poetic and musical in tone. Friday was the custom in Italian neighborhoods to eat fish based on our Catholic Religion and it was a day of abstinence.

When he stopped by my Grandmother's candy story, he was bombarded with many women shopping for various seafood for the evening meal. I was always happy to see him as he would always buy me an ice cream called "Mello Roll" and he would always let me hold the horses rein. I thought I was holding the horse at bay but actually the horse would only respond to his commands in Italian and my holding on tight to the reins was only a gesture.

This scenario went on for years, every Friday, until eventually we moved away and I never saw him again until one day, years later, a fisherman opened a seafood store on Court Street – one block from my home. My Mother had asked me to go buy some shrimp for her and when I entered the store I realized that this was the same "Phil the Fishman" who used to buy me ice cream in the old neighborhood. I asked him if he remembered buying me ice cream as a young boy and he was dumb-founded and could not believe that I remembered him. It really is a small world and small acts of kindness can make a huge and lasting impression in the mind of a child.

PLAYING SUPERMAN JUMPING OFF
GRANDMA'S CHICKEN COOP

My cousins, Louie Ciolina and Georgie VanCott were my playmates in my Grandmother's backyard. Our imaginations were unlimited. One day we would be cowboys, the next day maybe pirates.

After hearing Superman stories on the radio, we became the flying super boys. We would place a towel or any garment that we could wrap around our necks to look like capes. Next we needed someplace to fly from and Grandma's chicken coop was ideal and we could easily climb to the top of it. We took turns jumping off the chicken coop with our capes flying in the wind behind us. Each of us would give out a yell as we flew in the air. Our antics aroused all the chickens and they would fly around the coop making all kinds of noises as their feathers fluttered in the air.

The commotion would alert Grandma who would run out with her broom and shoo us off the coop. When we hit the ground we would roll over in the dirt where we once again became three little boys playing with towels around their neck instead of the powerful and fearless Superman emanating from the little box on the table in the kitchen – Up, Up and away! Faster than a speeding bullet!

MY TURN IN THE SINK

What I am about to relate in this short explanation would be impossible for kids and grand kids to comprehend.

From the day I was born in 1936 until 1947 we lived in a cold water flat with no heat or hot water. All heat in the winter was provided from a wood burning stove which was later replaced by a kerosene heater. Hot water was obtained by heating water in large pots which was used for both bathing and cooking and there was always a pot simmering on top of the stove.

With five children my Mother would have to bathe all of us one at a time in a large sink in the kitchen. This wasn't too bad during the hot summer months but during the cold winter months it was an ordeal. Trying to keep the kitchen warm enough so that we would not catch a cold was difficult. The bathing was quick and we were wrapped in towels immediately and dressed in record time.

Imagine maintaining a family under those conditions. Life in those days for the poor was a life and death struggle. Years later I discovered that my Grandmother had 16 children of which only 8 survived. Eight of them died from pneumonia.

WATCHING THE PUPPET SHOW AT ABRAHAM & STRAUSS DEPARTMENT STORE

During the 1940's Abraham and Strauss Department Store on Fulton Street in Brooklyn would have various puppet shows in their front window. This was a way of attracting families to the department store.

Special Christmas shows were performed depicting Christmas stories. At other times there would be various scenes including The Three Bears, Little Red Riding Hood or the Three Little Pigs – all of which fascinated all of the children.

The sidewalk would be lined with kids and parents, intently watching these puppets as they acted out the story. When a villain appeared the children in synchronized tones would express a boooo sound. The show's were performed at various hours of the day and was enjoyed by all.

Depending on the expression on the faces of the children one could determine the mood of the scene, happy or sad. In those days entertainment was simple as their parents rushed them to a department store to see a show which brought such pleasure at no cost to the family.

LISTENING TO ALL THE STORIES THESE OLD ITALIAN MEN CAME UP WITH

I think every neighborhood had a collection of old men who would sit and play cards, dominoes and checkers; all while smoking cigars and drinking demitasse coffee or a good glass of red wine.

I would listen to these men with their magnificent stories which were endless and exciting to a seven year old boy. One day the discussions would be about who was the greatest opera singer – Enrico Caruso or Mario Lanza. The discussions would last for hours with each man telling his own personal experience. One of my favorites was how General Garibaldi unified Italy in the 1860's.

The stories could change instantly going from opera to how the wars were won depending on who had control of the conversation. I was fascinated with all the different stories.

My Mother would say to me, "Stay away from all those geeps!"

My Mother had some of the funniest expressions and it seemed that she had just the right one for most any occasion.

During the summer of 1944, I found an old discarded table in my grandfather's backyard. I came up with the idea of converting it into an airplane. With a couple of 2x4's for the wings and a 2x6 for the seating area, I nailed these boards together for my new airplane.

I borrowed my Grandmother's pasta colander for a metal helmet and a broken baby carriage wheel as my steering system.

Next my cousin Ronnie Ciolino and I climbed aboard and our imagination took us to all the places our minds could come up with. We flew over the rooftops , New York Harbor, Statue of Liberty and finally we decided to fly off to Coney Island. All of these imaginary places came to life without leaving Grandma's backyard on Hamilton Avenue.

100

WIPING OFF MY AUNTS SLOPPY WET KISSES, ROUGE, LIPSTICK AND THE SMELL OF TOILET WATER

No one will ever know how I dreaded seeing my Aunts coming to visit us as I knew what was in store. No matter how hard I tried to hide from them they always found me.

My parents taught us to kiss our Aunts and they would make certain that this punishment was inflicted on us. First of all I was a very skinny and undernourished looking kid and I feared for my life! As soon as they spotted me they would immediately attack me and give me a bear hug which almost crushed me. The duration of these bear hugs were quite lengthy and I almost suffocated in their large, over weight body. My face turned beet red as they squeezed me between their large bosoms and I disappeared between the folds of their body before they finally released me. Next came the onslaught of those dreaded, sloppy wet kisses. Over and over and over.

By the time they finished I was covered with lipstick marks all over my face. In those days the women wore so much makeup – face powder, rouge and of course lots of lipstick and they splashed toilet water all over their body which had a nasty smell. The odor was so strong that it gave me a headache.

As soon as they released me I would immediately begin wiping everything from my face as everyone laughed hilariously.

GETTING SUZIE'S DOG MAD

Playing in our backyard everyday became like a nursery as well as a playground under the watchful eye of both my Mother and Grandmother.

One day our next door neighbor's dog barked and tried to jump the fence as though he wanted to kill us. The louder we shouted for him to stop the more enraged he became. Later in life we found out that the dog only understood Italian. By us shouting at him the dog took that as an act of aggression. Thank God for the fence which protected us or I believe he would have ripped us apart.

Once we found a hole in the fence and we poked a broomstick into the hole. The dog would bite the other end of the stick while we held on tightly to our end. The tug of war was fun for us but agitating to the dog. While this commotion was going on, our neighbor, Suzie was watching the action. She would yell down from her window, "You are afraid of my dog?" I shouted back, "Your dog is trying to bite me!" to which she replied, "I'll come down and show you he doesn't bite.

While she was on her way down we stuck the broom back into the hole but we did not realize that he was waiting there with his mouth open and the broom went right into his mouth and the dog went berserk and let out a death screeching howl.

SUZIE FERRIOLA GETTING BIT BY HER OWN DOG

By the time Suzie got down the dog was raving mad and ready to attack anything that came within striking distance. Before she had a chance to say a word the dog attacked her and bit into her backside and would not turn loose. All hell broke loose in her yard as her Mother came out screaming and cursing in Italian. Next came her Father with a horse whip while laying into his own dog and cursing, using words I had heard only from my Grandfather when he was upset.

We were completely shocked and dumbfounded and did not utter a word as we watched all the commotion going on. Moments later her brother rushed her to Long Island College Hospital where she required medical treatment.

Years later, even after she was married with a family of her own we would both laugh at the situation which happened when we were young although it was not funny when it happened.

EASTER BUNNY MAN, A TRUE ACT OF KINDNESS

A few houses down from our home lived an old man, alone in one of the top floor apartments. He would leave for work very early in the morning and the only time we would see him was in the evening. Regardless of how tired he was, he would always greet us kids with a smile and give us a few small pieces of candy.

When the Easter Holiday came along he could be seen coming home from work with two large shopping bags. He would greet us with a, "Happy Easter!" while he reached into his bag and brought out a large chocolate bunny rabbit for each of us. Each Bunny had a ribbon wrapped around its neck and it looked very festive. One could never imagine the impact this had on my sister and I as candy, especially such a large bunny had on our lives with his gift of kindness to the poor children in our Red Hook neighborhood.

He would smile and slowly shuffle off to his top floor apartment with an expression of satisfaction on his face.

As he approached us the women would yell to us, "Here comes the il-chicolato omo!"

I later figured out that he must have been the chocolate maker at one of the many nearby chocolate factories in the neighborhood.

104

GOING OFF TO WAR TO FIGHT THE GERMANS AND JAPS

During the 1940's we created scenes from our imagination using household items as our weapons and helmets as we pretended to fight the war with the Germans and Japanese.

The war was something we created in our imaginations as a game to be played while the weekly newsreels in the local theatre hit home with our parents and other families nearby as sons and daughters fought the reality of a terrible time in our history.

AUNT AGGIE BURNING HER BUTT

My Aunt Aggie had a habit where each morning during the cold winter mornings of rolling out of bed and coming into my Mother's kitchen where she would back up to the stove and lift the back of her dress and get as close to the stove as possible.

On this particular morning she was still half asleep when she accidently got too close to the stove and burned her backside. Then suddenly everyone was startled by her loud scream as she jumped into the air while running around the kitchen table. My Mother was running behind her trying to throw cold water on her backside. Her underwear was burned and so was her backside. We tried to laugh, but my Mother gave us the evil eye while motioning to us that she would kill us if we did.

That ended the habit of Aunt Aggie backing up to the stove to keep warm.

"AUNT AGGIE BURNING HER BUTT"   Phil Frazer

LEST WE FORGET | SUGAR SPILL AT HICKS ST. & HAMILTON AVE.

From the beginning of World War II, many foods were rationed and each family had to have a book of coupons in order to purchase the necessities of everyday living.   Meat, milk and other grocery items were purchased using coupons, including sugar.

One morning, a Domino Sugar truck loaded with bags of sugar was trying to go up the incline of Hicks Street from Hamilton Avenue. Suddenly, a cable broke and bags of sugar fell from the truck spilling sugar onto the streets as the bags broke open from the impact.

The next scene was something which could only be imagined by those who suffered thru those difficult times or from newsreels seen of a war devastated Europe.

Every Mother on the block gave their kids coffee pots, large cooking pots, buckets, kettles or anything else that could hold sugar. There we were, looking like scavengers scooping up sugar and running home with our treasure. Back and forth came the kids like ants running back and forth scooping every bit of sugar they could.

Looking back I realized just how poor and desperate the people were to feed their large families and the people of the neighborhood. I had a cup and a pasta pot to put the sugar I collected into. The scene looked like a scene after the war was over in devastated Germany.

Yes! This happened right here in the USA in Brooklyn, New York during my childhood.

"Who Ate the ends of The Italian Bread?" The BAKER GAVE it to me This WAY — HA ·HA

WHO ATE THE ENDS OF THE ITALIAN BREAD? | THE BAKER GAVE IT TO ME THIS WAY

Take my word for it. Caputo's Italian Bakery on Court Street in Brooklyn was the greatest bakery around. My Mother would send me there to pick up a few loaves of bread. The aroma of fresh baked bread right out of the oven was a temptation no young boy could resist.

During my long 3 block walk home I would start to nibble at the ends of the bread sticking out of the bag. Most of the time the bread would arrive home with the ends missing and my mother would ask, "Who ate the ends off the bread?" My answer was always the same, "That's how Caputo gave them to me!" We would both laugh; it was just a little fun between a mother and son.

BRINGING MY FATHER LUNCH WHILE SOLDIERS MARCHED DOWN 58TH STREET AT BROOKLYN ARMY BASE TO WAITING SHIPS BOUND FOR EUROPE | 1941 WWII

During the early stages of World War II, my Father worked as a longshoreman at the Brooklyn Army Base located at 58th Street in Brooklyn. They loaded the transport ships with airplanes, ammunition, tanks and of course thousands of US Troops who were being deployed to Europe.

Many days my Mother and I would travel to the Army Base to bring my Father some lunch. I was absolutely fascinated by how many tanks and planes that covered every available space within the Army base compound. I would look thru the iron fence and see airplanes swaying in the air, attached to cables as they were lowered into the holes of the cargo ships.

My train of thought was broken by a sergeant or group leader yelling instructions for the men to march. The line of troops was as far up to 58th street in a sea of human soldiers marching down toward the waterfront. Their movement appeared like ants while boarding the ships and the activity of men moving so fast in every direction.

I was too young to understand the significance of it all and I yearned to march with the soldiers. Little did I know that some of them were touching the US soil for the very last time.

On a trip to the Brooklyn Army Base in the 1960's, Senator Robert F. Kennedy along with ILA President Buddy Scotto, were flanked by my Father Salvatore Bracco on the right with my Uncle George VanCott directly behind my father and to the left of Senator Kennedy was my Uncle Thomas Bracco and another era was about to come to an end.

I had an Uncle Sammy who raced homing pigeons. He lived on the corner of Smith Street and Union and on top of his roof was a large pigeon coop. His son, Louie and I were allowed to sit on the roof and feed and water the birds. He would comb the sky looking for stray pigeons. As soon as he spotted one he would go into action. No stray could fly within eye sight of Smith and Union Street without him observing their flight pattern. He would rapidly open his coop and with a long bamboo pole with a red flag on it he would release all of his pigeons into the air.

The birds would run their normal circle flight pattern with him waving the birds on. Soon the stray birds would fly into the pattern of his pigeons. Next he would call his birds' home by depositing feed by his coop. Slowly, each bird would return home to eat, bringing the new birds with them.

He would then pluck the feathers of the new bird and place it into a coop until its feathers grew back. By that time the bird had become adjusted to his new home and to Uncle Sammie's pigeons.

THE DAY PRESIDENT ROOSEVELT STOPPED BY GRANDMA'S CANDY STORE

During the 1930's, President Franklin D. Roosevelt made a tour of New York, and to Red Hook . The Red Hook Projects were first built as a Federal Works Program initiative under former President Franklin Delano Roosevelt and probably accounted for his visit to our neighborhood. This occurred before I was born, however, I heard the story over and over from my Grandmother.

His tour took him thru the city and into Brooklyn where his motorcade stopped in front of Grandma's candy store at 190 Hamilton Avenue. People from all over the neighborhood gathered in front of her candy store in order to greet the President.

My Grandmother being an Italian immigrant never got over the fact that the President of the United States stopped by her candy store. He took the time to shake hands with her and many of her neighbors. This impression lasted throughout her life and she never forgot it. It was told to me so often that I almost feel that I was there.

HIDING FROM AUNT SUZIE | RED HOOK POOL

Thank God for the Red Hook Pool down on Bay Street in Brooklyn. It was constructed during the late 1930's as part of a reconstruction project to create jobs and to stimulate the economy.

This was the only real recreation for us poor kids in Red Hook. During the summer, my cousins Louie, Georgie and I would spend countless days swimming at this Department of Parks swimming Pool. Each day brought on different challenges from each other like, "Can you swim the length of the pool? Can you swim underwater the width of the pool?" As a result we became excellent strong swimmers and it became a daily routine during the hot summer days where little other relief could be found from the heat.

Being outdoors most of the time, the color of our skin became dark brown. On this particular day my Aunt Suzie came looking for us since she was ready to go home. We were having so much fun playing that we drifted into a large group of black children.

We then noticed our Aunt Suzie walking right by us while calling out our names but we blended in so well that she could not even spot us. Each time she circled the length of the pool we would lower our bodies into the water with only our eyes showing . While we were in the water laughing she was walking around in sheer panic screaming out our names.

The funniest part of the entire episode was that her son was less than 4 feet away from her. Each trip around, her yelling and screaming became louder and louder until finally a black kid snitched on us and we were captured. On the way home we were laughing hysterically while my aunt shouted in frustration, "Just wait until I get you home!"

NOT EVEN THE SAINTS ARE SAFE IN THIS HOUSE

One winter morning my grandmother from New Jersey came to visit us. My Mother would keep a large cooking pot of water on a wood burning stove which was used for bathing and cooking. Grandma was always fearful of me and was never at ease because of all the crazy situations I would get into. Mother and Grandmother were in the kitchen talking while I was in my Mother's bedroom. I was completely mesmerized by the lighted candle which she kept on her dresser. On the dresser was also a statue of Saint Anthony and next to it was a red glass with a candle in it which was glowing softly.

My mother had a plastic comb which I started to pass over the flames slowly and to my amazement the flame would follow the comb in any direction in which I moved it. Suddenly the comb caught fire and my reaction was to throw it away. The comb hit her dresser and bounced onto her bed. The dresser which had a white doily on it caught fire. The comb fell onto the bed and it caught fire as well.

Both ladies went into a panic and my Mother, in desperation grabbed the pot of hot water and extinguished the fire on both the bed and the dresser. My Grandmother was holding onto her heart for she was prone to having anxiety attacks frequently for no apparent reason.

She immediately grabbed her belongings and purse as she ran down the stairs and onto the street. She was shouting to my Mother, "I am going back to Jersey since not even the Saints are safe in this house."

Months went by before she came back to visit and even then she was never at ease

114

Both my sister Bridget and I met Santa Claus at a very young age. We found out later that our Father's friend, named Pennock, was the guy dressed up as Santa. On one cold winter night he appeared at my mother's kitchen, as the curtains were blowing out the window into the night air.

We were both mesmerized with him and he gave us one toy each since he had just enough toys to go around for all the other boys and girls in the neighborhood. As he climbed out the window he told us he would give us a ride on his sleigh next year. As he climbed up the fire escape ladder to the roof of our house, our neighbors dog began howling and barking. Our next-door neighbor Mr. Ferriola, in a loud voice, screamed into the night air "What is going on?" and of course all of this was in Italian. His wife Margaret was telling him to go to bed! It's only Santa Claus.

Both Bridget and I waited year after year but he never appeared again and our chance of a ride on his sleigh vanished with our memories.

After all these years I keep looking but am beginning to wonder if he's really coming!

GETTING EVEN WITH THE COP

My cousin Sal Acello and I would always play on our block where at the end of our street was a pool hall named Abe's. We were too young to realize that it was not a good place for us to play near. Each day at 4 o'clock the police shifts would change and one particular policeman would walk down the street twirling his night stick in the air. He would go out of his way to hit us in the backside and tell us to go home. We would tell him "We live on this block" but to no avail and he would chase us anyway. Finally my cousin said "We will get even with him." Each day when he started his shift he would stop and read the newspaper at my Grandmothers newsstand.

Sal came with a cooking pan and we climbed to the top of the roof. Next we put some water in the pan and our goal was to throw the water down on his head. We watched him from the rooftop until he got directly below us. Sal told me to carry the pan of water close to the edge. He then grabbed a handful of roofing gravel and put it in the pan. I tried to get down on my knees so I could see better but I lost my footing and the whole pan with all of its contents rained down onto the Policeman's head.

We both got scared and I climbed down into my apartment and ran directly to my bedroom. Sal ran along the rooftops and climbed down someone's fire escape, jumped over a fence and disappeared somewhere on Columbia Street.

Up came the policeman along with my Mother, my Grandmother and neighbors as he drew his gun while telling my Uncle to open the roof access. Up to the roof they went. My Mother held her door open just slightly so she and I could see what was going on.

Our revenge was pulled off without anyone getting in trouble as the two phantoms struck again.

116

JOHNNY IS ABOUT TO GET A SNOWBALL ON HIS HEAD | BLIZZARD 1947

Johnny is about to get hit on the head with a large snowball as we play in the huge snowdrifts which had accumulated in a recent snowfall.

SHOVELING GRANDMA'S DRIVEWAY

RED HOOK POOL 1940'S

On hot summer evenings our family would go for a walk after dinner which usually led us to the Red Hook Swimming Pool. It was very hot during those summer evenings and we couldn't wait to get there. I would run up the concrete steps which led to the observation deck. Here I would hold onto the iron bars and look at all the people cooling off in the pool.

It was magical to us because at night the overhead lights would shine on the water and mix with the pool lights producing an iridescent array of colors which shimmered across the water. Blue, green, yellow and all combinations as the colors seemed to be jumping around in the water. This was due to the rippling of the water by so much activity going on.

There was always a cool breeze and the smell of chlorine in the pool created a clean and cooling aroma in the air. We were told that when we got older we would be able to go swimming in the pool at night but only with an adult.

At the base of the concrete steps there was always a Good Humor vendor and occasionally our parents would buy us an orange drink or an ice cream. We would enjoy our treat while returning to the heat of our apartment.

118

The death rate in those cold water flats was very high and I almost became a victim. I contracted pneumonia and was being treated by Dr. Louis Gentile of 3rd Place in Brooklyn.

Whenever someone was sick, Dr. Gentile would come to your home regardless of what the hour was. He always carried a small black leather bag and he was very impressive and a positive person. My illness kept getting worse until it was diagnosed as double pneumonia. He soon realized that the medicine I was taking was combating each other. I was rushed to Kings County Hospital at once. I can still remember my Grandmother pulling the bedspread from her bed and wrapping me in it.

In the emergency room I sat there limp as the doctors gave me three injections. Concern was evident on my parent's faces as the doctors took over and started working on me. I spent 30 days in the hospital before I was released. For the first time I tasted white bread and butter and the doctors told them to give me all that I wanted.

AUNT BETTY BEING ATTACKED BY GRANDMA'S ROOSTER

One day in the backyard Grandma's prize rooster decided to pitch a fit for no apparent reason. My Aunt Betty was the closest one around so it attacked her with full force. She ran around the yard trying to get away but he would run her down and jump at her face. She jumped up on a picnic table and was screaming for dear life when my Father heard her and came running down with a broomstick and hit the rooster until it retreated into the chicken coop.

We were all baffled by its behavior and never figured out what caused him to go wild but perhaps it was the color of her dress.

NEIGHBORHOOD ACTIVITY - THE KNIFE SHARPENER AND THE RAGMAN

Each neighborhood had weekly visits from the ragman, scissor sharpener, vendors selling fruits and vegetables and other items needed for their daily life in the early 40's.

120

WORLD WAR II AIR RAIDS

The air raids of World War II created anxiety, uncertainty and fear for many of the individuals along the East Coast including New York. Many nights my Mother would wake us from a deep sleep and whisper to us to be very quiet. She slowly led us to our bedroom window in total darkness so we could observe what was happening.

Spotlights could be seen combing the night sky in almost every direction as sirens screamed away into the night.

We were taught to place our clothes and shoes next to the bed at night and to be able to dress in the dark. With a concerned look on my Mother's face as her eyes darted back and forth over the activity going on outside our window we realized the significance of the situation.

The Air Defense Warden would run up and down the street shouting to anyone who had their lights on. Behind us in the dark was always my Grandmother praying with her rosary beads.

From our top floor window we could see all of lower Manhattan business buildings as their lights were extinguished, one by one until it was total darkness. Looking out to the opposite side of the street we could see other families peeking out of their windows also. Everyone sat waiting patiently for the all clear signal.

Finally the all clear signal sounded and people tried to get back to sleep as best they could. This scenario became a way of life for the residents of our neighborhood during World War II.

MY GRANDFATHER - FILIPPO BRACCO
IN HIS BACKYARD BOCCE COURT

My Grandfather had his own Bocce Court in his back yard. He was a legend in his time as being the best Bocce player in New York.

Many tournaments were arranged by different Bocce Clubs and Gamblers and were played in his back yard. Some of the best players from Italy came to Brooklyn just to play against him hoping to beat him. He was known as Don Filippo of South Brooklyn.

When I was very young I would spend hours with him, raking his court. I loved rolling the small Bocce Balls since I was able to hold it in my small hands. I could not grip the larger balls so I would kick them along with my foot. This brought laughter to my Grandfathers face.

I can still remember the first time I saw a guitar and heard it being played. It was at night in his backyard with a crowd of people with a man singing and playing his guitar. Years later I learned that the man singing and playing was the famous Italian singer, Carlo Butti.

My Grandmother told me that large sums of money were wagered on these tournaments. At the end of the tournament everyone would drink wine and sing Italian songs into the night as Grandma and my aunts cooked dinner for everyone.

RAKING GRANDPA'S BOCCE COURT

Grooming the Bocce Court was an every day job and I was thrilled to be able to help Grandpa maintain it as I loved watching the tournaments which were frequently held here.

FUTURE BROOKLYN DODGER GRANDPA'S BACKYARD BOCCE COURT | 1941

All dressed and ready to go with my Dad and Uncle Mimi to see the Brooklyn Dodgers celebrate the winning of the National League Championship in 1941 at Borough Hall in Brooklyn.

MY COLLAR WAS 2 SIZES TOO SMALL FOR MY CONFIRMATION

My Confirmation turned out to be a grand commotion which turned the entire house into a panic. I told my Mother that I was not going to let the Bishop slap me in the face. This started a chain of family members each giving me their version of what would happen. All of my clothes were ready except that I did not have a white shirt. Everyone was running around hoping to make sure everything came off without a hitch. My mother made arrangements for us to be at the Natoli Photo Studio at a certain time.

Off they ran to Columbia Street to get me a white shirt at the very last minute. They could not find a shirt in my size and in desperation they took a size smaller.

Dressing me for this event was a fiasco since I could not stop fidgeting with my too tight collar and my tie was choking me. At the ceremony my entire family was in the back of the church praying that all would go well.

The Bishop must have had mercy on me since I was the only kid choking and unable to breath. His slap was a love tap and the Confirmation was achieved without incident. Off to the photographer we went for more punishment.

OUR PLAYGROUND - THE ROOF TOPS OF HAMILTON AVE.

Both my cousin Tuddi and I spent many a day climbing from one roof top to another. We often ate our lunch on the rooftops of Hamilton Avenue. From our bird's eye view we could see all the activity going on in the New York Harbor. The loud sounds of tug boats pushing large ships around and maneuvering them into the various piers along the waterfront could be heard from where we were on the rooftop. We could see the US Naval ships coming in for repairs on their way to the Brooklyn Navy Yard.

We could see the Statue of Liberty which was in our direct view and we enjoyed watching the Ferry Boats coming and going back and forth from Brooklyn to New York with some going to Staten Island.

The air was full of activity. Seagulls and Pigeons were flying about while looking for a meal. I really got excited when I saw a large aircraft carrier with damaged decks and scars of a Navy sea battle. Tuddi was always on the lookout for Naval Submarines with their periscopes standing out against the blue sky. All the large buildings in the area had large anti aircraft guns mounted on the rooftops and spotlights which would comb the night air during an air raid. Sometimes during the day, sirens would scream out and we knew we had to get home immediately. Everything would come to a quiet standstill as everyone in the city waited for the all clear signal.

We were impressed with the enormous size of one particular aircraft gun which was mounted on the Sapolin Paint Factory in Red hook and we always wished we could hear it fire. This was a very exciting and educational playground for many of us in those days.

A DAY WITH THE BROOKLYN DODGERS AND MEETING JACKIE ROBINSON

After winning the competition at The Happy Felton Knot Hole Gang at Ebbetts field, I was invited into the Dodger's dugout to meet all of the players. They all autographed my baseball and gave me a glove and a bat.

Jackie Robinson told me that he was watching the competition and said he was very impressed with my ability. You can imagine that I was on cloud nine after that comment he made which was televised and all my friends and family were watching including a large group of Longshoremen from the Brooklyn Army Base.

During the TV Show Peewee Reese was the player I wanted most to ask questions of. After a few baseball strategy questions he said "This kid will take over my shortstop position in the future."

When I returned home to my neighborhood it seemed like all Brooklyn was waiting to congratulate me. What an experience for a young, dedicated Brooklyn Dodger fan!

GETTING A SHELLACKING

My Father gave me the worst beating or shellacking as it was known in those days. It was so severe that I was unable to go to school or to even sit for two days.

The reason for the beating was that one day after school me and my friend Johnny Ferriola would go down to his father's horse stable on West 9th Street where Johnny would hook up a horse to his father's vegetable wagon and we would ride down the street towards Public School 27. While Johnny drove, I would climb under the wagon like the cowboys did on the silver screen. The kids in the neighborhood would cheer us on, to our delight and we became even more daring. An observer approached my Father and told him that one day his son would be killed by the crazy stunts he was performing with the horse and wagon.

My Father staked himself out at the stable to wait for us to hitch up the horses that afternoon and he asked for an explanation. I guess it wasn't good enough because he beat me from West 9th Street all the way home to Hamilton Avenue. As we approached the police station I felt sure that the cops would save me but they simply turned their backs and did nothing.

When my Grandfather heard what had happened he intervened and told my Father that he never ever wanted to hear of him hitting me again.

I can only imagine the fear that gripped my father as his concern mounted over my safety. Today, this man whom I loved dearly would have been arrested for child abuse instead of concern for the life of his child.

THE PARK (DEPT. OF PARKS) | BROOKLYN, NY 1945

The water fountain was a frequent stop for us as we ran and romped through Carroll Park in the heat of the summer.

CHINESE LAUNDRY

A Chinese Laundry Owner scaring my mother and her Sister (1915, approximately). They would chant a song in Italian about Chinese men had long hair and braids. A lesson Learned!

128

ITALIAN FEAST MARCHING BAND

Each year the various Catholic Churches would have a feast for their patron saints.

It was more of a large block party with good food, dancing, music and games. The entire neighborhood got involved and each family sold some kind of food specialty such as, sausages with peppers and onions, calzones, pizzas, zeppellas and of course pastries.

My Mother and Grandparents enjoyed the Italian singers and comedy acts. The Italian love songs were their favorite and they knew every word as they sang loudly along with the crowd. The excitement and roar of the crowd would reach a feverish pitch as the Italian Feast Marching Band came down the street in colorful uniforms and their music was so loud that it hurt my ears.

Some of the musicians played off key but that did not matter. Being so close to the band I had to hold my ears to keep from going deaf. The Grand Finale was of course the Italian National Anthem and with this the fireworks would roar into the darkness of the sky.

The pageantry, lights, music, dancing and the smell of good food cooking filled the air with the finest aromas as they melded together to make a lasting impression which remains with me today.

MOTHER SAYS "ACT LIKE MUMMIES IN SOMEONE'S HOME" | FIVE PERFECT MUMMIES

In those years, kids were to be seen and not heard. It was very embarrassing for parents if their children were unruly either at home or especially at someone else's home. If we had to visit a friend or relative we were given explicit instructions on how to behave. Mother would tell us, "After you greet everyone, go sit down on the couch and don't move. If they offer you something to eat or drink, you say no thank you unless I say it's ok. I want you kids to act like Mummies – as a matter of fact, five perfect mummies and if you don't you will get it when you get home." If by chance I might have touched or looked at some item they had on their table, I could expect a quick twist of my ears. All of this occurred of course while the host was not looking.

My poor brother Frank, in his youth had his ears twisted so often that they extended out from his head and mine were constantly red. Eventually they returned to normal as we learned never to do anything my Mother told us not to do.

There we were, the five perfect mummies sitting on the couch in our relatives home and they would often say "These kids are so well behaved. Are they alright?" Over the years as we reminisced about those days we would laughingly call ourselves "the five mammalukes."

"Moving During The Blizzard 1947 Dad, Uncle Ralph & Me" Phil Bracco

MOVING DURING THE BLIZZARD | 1947

During the winter months of 1947 we were forced by the City of New York to move from Hamilton Avenue to make room for the construction of the Brooklyn Battery Tunnel. Finally we were able to move to 2nd place on the top floor in Grandma's four story brownstone house which she had recently purchased.

We were thrilled as well as amazed to be in a house where we had heat and hot and cold running water. Just as fate would have it we were the last house standing on the block and just three days after we moved the upper floors collapsed into the street. I guess someone was watching over our family with five kids.

The blizzard of 1947 hit New York City severely and every means of transportation was shut down. My parents faced a dilemma on how to move our meager belongings to another apartment while this storm loomed over the city. My Father, his brother Ralph and I moved all of our belongings on two snow sleds through the storm. I really can't remember how many trips it took but we did it.

Stomping thru the snow was an adventure for a little boy but the wind was so ferocious that we had to cover our eyes' with a scarf. I will never forget, when the final trip was completed, my grandmother had a hot meal waiting for everyone. The meal was a homemade hot beef stew and I can still remember that the vegetables and the beef were cut into such large chunks that I could hardly get them into my mouth.

The warmth of a heated apartment along with the hot meal and the family celebration of the move from Hamilton Avenue to the safety of a new start for our family was an experience I will never forget.

I have no idea how he learned how to hypnotize chickens but my Uncle Mikey did. We would gather in the yard and he would tell us kids to catch some chickens. We really liked the idea of chasing chickens in the backyard with feathers flying, chickens squawking while us kids were running and laughing.

When we brought the chickens to him he would then take a stick and draw a straight line in the dirt. Next he would hold the chicken down and position his head on the ground so that the chicken's eyes would be focused on the straight line. Within seconds the chicken laid on the ground in a total trance. It looked dead with no movement at all.

To bring them out of the trance he would flip them into the air. When they hit the ground they would be disoriented for a few seconds while running around in circles. All the kids would be laughing and rolling on the ground from the chickens behavior.

My Grandmother would come down with her broom and chase Uncle Mikey around the backyard while yelling for him to stop. In Italian she would say by him hypnotizing her chickens that they would forget how to lay eggs.

"Uncle Mike Hypnotizing Granma's chickens"
1940's Hamilton Ave   Phil Bracco

MOTHER, MARY, FRANK & THERESA ON STATEN ISLAND FERRY RIDE | EARLY 1950'S

The Staten Island Ferry was an occasional Sunday outing for our family as my parents struggled to find a different view of life for their children with very limited resources in those lean times of the history of our country.

THERESA, TELL THEM I'M YOUR GRANDFATHER

My sister Theresa, as a young child was very shy and if asked a question she would look directly to the ground and would not lift her head for anyone.

At this time she was in kindergarten and her class was to be over at 11 am. Normally my mother would walk those few blocks to PS 27 and meet her and they would walk home together. This was an everyday ritual.

On one of my grandfather's rare visits from New Jersey, my mother asked him to walk down and pick up Theresa. At 11 o'clock sharp, out came all of the children. Mrs. Donovan was waiting for my mother so when my grandfather approached and looked at Theresa saying "Hello Teressina" my sister put her head down and would not respond. Mrs. Donovan asked Theresa "Do you know this man" but Theresa did not respond. My Grandfather said to Theresa, in his broken English "Tell them I'm your Grandfather" but still no response.

Mrs. Donovan grabbed my Grandfather with one arm and Theresa with the other and proceeded to take them to the principal's office where they immediately called the police. They kept interrogating him but still Theresa would not say a word. Finally Mrs. Donovan remembered that I was in another class so she came and summoned me and said, "There is a man in our office saying he is Theresa's grandfather and that he is here to pick her up." Since my Grandfather in Brooklyn had recently died I replied, "that is impossible because my grandfather passed away," and this really poured fuel on the fire as she rushed back to the office with me to nab this kidnapper. Well needless to say my grandfather was happy to see me walk in the room as I explained that this was my grandfather from New Jersey.

After dropping her off at home he told my Mother, "this kid will put you in jail," as he immediately left for New Jersey and it was a long time before we saw grandpa come back to Red Hook for a visit with our family.

SISTER MARY DRINKING MILK

My sister Mary, as a baby would drink her milk from a Pepsi Cola bottle with a large nipple attached to the top. It seemed that every time you saw her she had that bottle in her hand. Just like any typical child you could find her in any position while drinking her milk. Sometimes she would lay on her back, other times almost upside down or with her legs in the air and any other contortion she could think of.

I often thought that it was probably because my mother could not afford a regular baby bottle that my sister drank milk from a soda bottle.

Whatever it was, my Mother had a hard time breaking Mary from the habit of carrying around that old Pepsi Cola Bottle.

SNOOZE IN FRONT OF GRAMMA'S CANDY STORE | 1936

Safe and secure as I slept in front of Grandma's candy store who could have imagined at that time that our life would be turned upside down within a few short years as World War II approached.

YOUNG FRANKIE BRACCO IN A SHOW DOWN WITH HOPALONG CASSIDY IN A&S DEPARTMENT STORE

During the era when Hopalong Cassidy was king he became the idol of all the young boys' in America including my small brother Frank.

All hell broke loose when it was announced that Hopalong Cassidy would appear in person at Abraham and Strauss Department Store at Fulton Street in Brooklyn with his horse Topper. I took Frank early on a Saturday morning and by the time we arrived the line of kids was around the department store about a block and a half long. With patience we finally got to see Hoppy and his horse and my brother had a thrill of a lifetime.

SOPHIA'S CHICKENS ESCAPING ON THE HUDSON TUBE

In those days when someone was sick, the family would bring live fresh chickens to the family of the ill patient. On this particular occasion my Grandmother in Jersey City New Jersey was ill and my mother sent her good friend Sophie and me with a shopping bag full of live chickens. The chicken's legs were tied and they were placed head first into the shopping bag.

Everything went fine until we sat down in the train headed for New Jersey via the Hudson Tubes. Suddenly the bag broke and live chickens went running, jumping and screaming all over the train car. Passengers began yelling and climbing up on their seats. I got scared and ran from them but Sophie was demanding that I help her catch them. Since she had no bags to put them in and not knowing how to contain them she wrung their necks as she caught them. This was a horrible scene not only to the passengers but to me as well as I had never experienced such a thing. Chicken feathers flew thru the air and finally floated slowly to the floor.

People were staring at us as we walked to Grandma's house as Sophie had me in one hand and the dead chickens in the other. Grandma got fresh killed chicken for her soup which was supposed to heal a person back to good health.

MY SISTER ACTING UP IN ST. STEVEN'S CHURCH

One Sunday morning in Saint Stevens Church on Hicks Street my sister Mary decided to act up during the 9 O'clock Mass. I tried everything I could in order to keep her quiet but to no avail.

The Priest, on the alter was saying the mass in Latin and of course most of the congregation was mostly elderly people. I made a big mistake when I told my sister Mary that the Saint to the left was watching her. Now she began making funny noises at the saints while the people close to us kept telling her to be quiet while making motions with their hands to their lips with a low shhhh sound.

The Priest was getting frustrated but no matter who spoke to her in a very calm voice she made these noises even louder. Each of the elderly ladies would take turns in their own way to make her stop but with no success. I finally took her hand and led her out of the church with the noises still coming out of her mouth. I guess that was one way to get out of going to church on Sunday.

While living on Hamilton Avenue, each New Year, my Grandfather would take all of the family children outside of the candy store where directly in front of the store was a steel pole that I believe was a Con Edison pole. To celebrate the New Year he would arm each of us with pots, pans and covers and he would use a hammer while hitting the steel pole which made a tremendous loud reverberating sound. All the kids would beat the pans together in celebration of the New Year.

This tradition was carried on even after my grandfather's death. For years later, on New Year's Eve my Father would take us down to Hamilton Avenue to beat on the same pole in order to keep this tradition alive. I believe he did it out of respect for his Father as he remembered the great joy he experienced with all the children and how his eyes lit up as we rang in the New Year together.

Sometimes, a few other people would walk by and greet us with good wishes for the New Year and we probably looked strange to them as we banged on the steel pole which was still standing on an otherwise desolate and destructed Hamilton Avenue.

As time passed my Father began to realize that times had changed and with it traditions were lost as a steel pole, where so many New Year's celebrations offered hope to our family at a time when there was no money for traditional noise makers, was destroyed to make room for the Brooklyn Battery Tunnel.

ONE AND ONLY DAY OUT WE SPEND WITH GRANDMA

I'll never forget the day my Grandmother closed the candy store in order to take my sister Bridget and I to Coney Island. As I grew into an adult it took on more significance to me as I realized what that meant financially to the family to lose a day's revenue but on this day, the trip to Coney Island with two of her Grandchildren was even more important.

PICNIC IN COFFEY PARK NEXT TO UNCLE MARIO'S STATUE

One of our favorite places for a picnic was in Coffee Park where we could see a statue of a soldier which we believed to be that of my Uncle Mario as we had heard many stories from my mother as she showed us pictures of him with a gun extended when he was in World War I.

LUNCH HOUR AT HAMILTON AVE.

From my fire escape perspective I was able to observe my environment while having my lunch, which usually consisted of an Italian Hero sandwich, which was washed down with a Coca Cola.

From this bird's eye view I was able to see people moving at different paces as they performed their daily chores. The sound of trolley bells off in the distant, ships in the harbor blowing their whistles and above my head 2 sea gulls flying dangerously close to me in hopes of getting some food scraps from my lunch.

The air was filled with activity, sounds, and smells of all kinds and at exactly 12 noon the factories would blow their whistles indicating that it was lunch time.

St. Stevens Church Bells would ring slowly one dong at a time for twelve dongs and it was officially 12 Noon.

"LUNCH HOUR at 190 HAMILTON AVE"
BROOKLYN, N. Y.

Phil Brecce

THREE ITALIAN LADIES AND A PARROT

These three fat ladies lived next door to each other. I guess they must have had very little house work to do because they spent most of the time sitting outside in front of their store. They had a table set up with a parrot who only understood Italian. On the table next to the parrot was a 5 gallon carboy filled with red wine. These ladies knew everyone's business and not a fly could go by without them knowing about it.

Each time I would walk by them each one would have advice for me. They would call me "Sonny Boy" and of course the parrot would repeat "sonny boy, sonny boy" over and over again. When the parrot wouldn't stop calling me one of the ladies would yell out in Italian, "stata zita faccieem," which translates to, "Shut your mouth you little bastard." And of course the parrot would then repeat, "faccieem, faccieem," over and over.

This was a real fiasco and they would give me a list of all the things I should not be doing such as, "don't go in the street, stay out of vacant lots, don't climb trees," and they would always end the conversation with, "How's your mother?"

Philly & Cousin Tuddy 1940's
EARLY 1940's
At the Foot of HAMILTON AVE, BROOKLYN, N.Y.

Phil Bracco

PHILLY & COUSIN TUDDI

Both my cousin Tuddi and I, when not in school could be seen roaming the waterfront piers in Red Hook Brooklyn. Many an hour was spent wondering how the rest of the world was and images raced through our minds filled with imagination.

It seemed like every tugboat captain along the waterfront knew us by name as they would blow the whistle to our delight. As we faced the New York waterfront harbor the Statue of Liberty was in our direct view which often seemed as though she was waving to us.

If you look far out to the right, I am sure you will still be able to see the ghosts of Tuddi and I as you get a glimpse of the Lady herself.

GRANDMA'S CHICKENS

Grandma's chickens were her pride and joy and she sat in her back yard observing them for long periods of time. But as old age set in her eyesight was so poor that she really could not determine whether it was a rooster or hen. Each day she would work her way down to the yard and open up the chicken coop. She would feel inside the nest with her hand and retrieve any eggs which the chickens had laid the night before. She would sometimes summon me to look into the dirt inside the chicken coop to see if she missed any eggs.

My Uncle Mike came up with a game plan so as not to disappoint her. He would take eggs from the ice box and roll them in the dirt, then place them in the nests. When she would gather the eggs she was so happy.

My Uncle Mike told me that she could not see and to prove it to me he said now watch this. He grabbed an old rooster and while she was sitting by her chicken coop he showed her the rooster and asked if he could kill it for our dinner. She quickly yelled at him and said, "No, no, no! That chicken lays at least 7 eggs a week."

We ran around the chicken coop where she could not see us and laughed hysterically.

COMING UP WITH A WILD STORY ON HOW THE WINDOW GOT BROKEN

LOOK AT THE BIRDIE - THAT'S ME

A roving photographer would visit our neighborhood taking pictures of children on a pony.

When they came to Grandma's candy store my mother hurriedly dressed me in my christening outfit for the photo session. The suit that I wore was my father's christening outfit and was later worn by my Grandson Eric and has been carefully placed back into our chest of treasures for the next generation.

"Look at The Birdie" That is me 1937 Brooklyn N.Y. Phil Bracco

Grandma's Candy Store Brooklyn, 1940's Phil Bracco

GRANDMA'S CANDY STORE

On hot summer days Grandma would wheel her tub of lemon ice to the front of the store as passersby would stop to refresh themselves.

To this day we cannot make a trip back to Brooklyn without first stopping at a local pastry shop to enjoy the refreshing cup of Lemon Ice even before we make it to my sister's home.

148

PICKING OUT CANDY IN GRAMMA'S CANDY STORE

My Grandfather called Bridget and I to the back of the store and gave us each a penny which we immediately took to the front candy counter where we would pick out our favorite candy and use our penny to pay Grandma for it. This made us feel like we were a paying customer and pleased that we could use our money to make a purchase. We felt important!

A penny went a long way in those days especially when your grandmother owned the store as she slipped extra pieces into our bag.

PAINLESS DENTIST

During my early years I never understood why people in the neighborhood feared going to a dentist. Then I received my dose of dental treatment at Columbia and Union Street. There was a dentist who most of the neighborhood went to at one time or another by the name of Dr. Weiss.

When the old time remedies failed Dr. Weiss was the last resort. Some of the archaic concoctions which were called treatments were pretty bad. For instance, putting whiskey on a toothache or an aspirin on an exposed tooth, and finally in desperation they would tie a string around the tooth and tie it to the kitchen door which was slammed shut with the hope that the tooth would come out. When all of these failed it was off to see Dr. Weiss.

When we reached the staircase leading to the second floor entrance we were shocked as a man came rushing down the steps while holding his jaw. This did not leave a good impression on my Mother. While sitting in the waiting room we could hear a person screaming in pain, yelling "No More! No More!" A few minutes later the patient came running out of the dentist chair right past us and down those metal steps and disappeared somewhere on Columbia Street.

Out came the nurse and said to me "You are next." My poor Mother was a nervous wreck by now. She didn't know whether to run or to go into the examination room. I finally went in and endured my limit of pain and punishment and on the way home my Mother called him every name in the book in Italian.

He was advertised as the painless dentist. Talk about false advertising.

150

FILTHY MONKEYS - LET'S GO

What a treat it was to go to the zoo at Prospect Park. On a late Sunday afternoon my Mother and Father would take us there and spend a leisurely day observing all of the animals. I would ask questions like "Why does an elephant put food under his chin?"

Mother loved to go to the bird house which had a large variety of different colored exotic birds.

I would run to the sea lions tank and was amazed at how they moved so quickly and the fun they seemed to have as they frolicked in the water. Then it was off to the Lions House where when you entered, the loud roar of the lions would echo off the walls and everyone became quiet and a little nervous. The lions would pace back and forth over and over again as they roared ferociously.

The monkey house was my favorite since they could jump, climb and swing for hours. My mother was very serious about not exposing her children to anything dirty. On this particular day the monkeys were wild and began throwing feces at the people observing. This made my mother upset but when they began to have sex with each other she tried to shield our eyes and shoved us away exclaiming "Those filthy monkeys! Let's go home." We were escorted out of the zoo immediately. Any questions I had, met with total silence.

151

LITTLE SISTER, BIG SISTER

Caring for the younger children in the family was something we all had a responsibility for and seeing that they got to school safely was one of those responsibilities.

"TERRY IN PROSPECT PARK"

Phil Bracco

Phil Bracco

TERRY IN PROSPECT PARK

All bundled up on a cold fall day, my sister Theresa, skating to the Prospect Park Oval skating arena which is outdoors. This was one of the free areas where the local children were able to go for recreation.

PLAYING 'BUCK, BUCK HOW MANY HORNS ARE UP'

Playing 'Buck, Buck, how many horns are up' was just one of
the great street games of the neighborhood which we played
frequently. We always searched for a fat kid to be the pillow boy.

BRIDGET AND PHILLY

A big sister helping her young brother get a cool drink from the water fountain in Coffee Park

RUNNING THROUGH COFFEY PARK

Running carefree through Coffey Park, oblivious to the turmoil which surrounded us

SWINGING IN CARROLL PARK

Swinging in the summer breeze is as popular today as it was then as all children from generation to generation still thrill to the feeling of the wind blowing in their faces as they swing back and forth.

OILING MY GLOVE FOR A BIG GAME

MOM AND DAD IN THE BACK YARD

As the years passed and we became teenagers my parents decided it was time to make another move and purchased a brand new brick home in Bensunhurst which was a stark contrast to what we had been accustomed to. The Bocce Court had been replaced by a Rose Garden which was my father's pride and joy. One era came to an end as another took it's place as we graduated from high school and eventually married and started a family of our own.

However the days spent growing up in Red Hook, where family and friends made up the entire neighborhood and "Where everybody knew your name", were embedded in my memories to last a lifetime.

YOU TRY IT FIRST GRANDPA - OKAY?

Some things never change as my granddaughter
Madison now does the same thing with me.

We hope you enjoyed Life On The Stoop. Stop on by our blog to let us know your thoughts and enjoy more unique art from Phil Bracco.

 www.LifeOnTheStoop.com

 www.facebook.com/LifeOnTheStoop

 www.twitter.com/LifeOnTheStoop

Made in the USA
Lexington, KY
10 December 2011